The Wild Side of Pet
Lizards

Jo Waters

Chicago, Illinois

For information, address the publisher:
Raintree, 100 N. LaSalle, Suite 1200, Chicago, IL 60602

Customer Service: 888-363-4266
Visit our website at www.raintreelibrary.com

Printed and bound in China by South China Printing Company.
08 07 06 05 04
10 9 8 7 6 5 4 3 2 1

Library of Congress Cataloging-in-Publication Data
Waters, Jo.
  The wild side of pet lizards / Jo Waters.
      p. cm. -- (The wild side of pets)
Includes bibliographical references (p.   ).
Contents: Was your pet lizard once wild? -- What types of lizards are there? -- Where do lizards come from? -- Lizard habitats -- Lizard anatomy -- How do lizards use their senses? -- How do lizards move? -- What do lizards eat? -- Hunting and handling -- Do lizards live in groups? -- Do lizards sleep? -- Life cycle of lizards -- What problems do lizards have?
  ISBN 1-4109-1022-9 (lib. bdg.-hardcover) -- ISBN 1-4109-1162-4 (pbk.)
  1. Lizards as pets--Juvenile literature. 2. Lizards--Juvenile literature. [1. Lizards as pets. 2. Lizards. 3. Pets.] I. Title.
  II. Series: Waters, Jo. Wild side of pets.
  SF459.L5W38 2004
  639.3'95--dc22
                              2003027729

Acknowledgments
The author and publisher would like to thank the following for permission to reproduce photographs:
pp. 4, 29 Photodisc; p. 5 top Alain Compost/Bruce Coleman Collection; p. 5 bot. Joe McDonald/Bruce Coleman Collection; p. 6 Stephen Dalton/ NHPA; p. 7 Getty Images; pp. 9, 11, 19, 21, 23, 25 Tudor Photography/Harcourt Education Ltd; p. 10 Photodisc/Getty Images; p. 12 D. Heuclin/ NHPA; p. 13 J. Watt/Bruce Coleman Collection; p. 14 M. Harvey/NHPA; p. 15 D Kjaer/Nature Picture Library; p. 16 B. Coster/NHPA; p. 17 Dr. Darlyne A. Murawski/Getty Images; p. 20 P. Lilja/Getty Images; p. 22 Corbis; p. 24 Minden Pictures; p. 26 B. Kenney/Oxford Scientific Films; p. 27 Densey Clyne Productions/Oxford Scientific Films; p. 28 Animals Animals/Oxford Scientific Films.

Cover photograph of a bearded dragon reproduced with permission of Tudor Photography/Harcourt Education Ltd. Inset cover photograph of Mediterranean chameleon reproduced with permission of John & Sue Buckingham/NHPA.

The publishers would like to thank Michaela Miller for her assistance in the preparation of this book.

Every effort has been made to contact copyright holders of any material reproduced in this book. Any omissions will be rectified in subsequent printings if notice is given to the publishers.

Contents

Some words are shown in bold, **like this.** You can find out what they mean by looking in the Glossary.

Was Your Pet Once Wild?

You may think that you just have a pet lizard, but really you have a wild animal living in your house. Finding out more about how your pet lives in the wild will help you give it a better life.

Lizards are **reptiles.** They are all **cold-blooded.** This means that their bodies are at the same temperature as their surroundings. They use the sun or the shade to warm up or cool down.

Iguanas are mostly found in North and South America.

Wild lizards are the same as the lizards we keep as pets. They are not like other pets. Lizards need special conditions and care to keep them healthy.

Make sure you find out as much as you can before you decide if a lizard is the right pet for you.

Have you got room?

Some lizards can grow to over 3 feet in their first year. As they get older, growth slows but never completely stops.

The Komodo Dragon is the world's largest lizard. It can grow to over 9 feet long and weigh up to 300 pounds.

Types of Lizard

There are more than 4,700 different **species** of lizard. These include tiny lizards that are insect-eaters, and really big meat-eaters.

The main species of lizard are iguanas, chameleons, geckos, gila monsters, monitors, and skinks. Monitor lizards were probably one of the first species of lizard alive on the Earth.

Lizard relatives

*Lizards are related to snakes. They are all **reptiles.** All reptiles are **cold-blooded,** have scaly skin, and forked tongues. Alligators, crocodiles, salamanders, and turtles are also reptiles.*

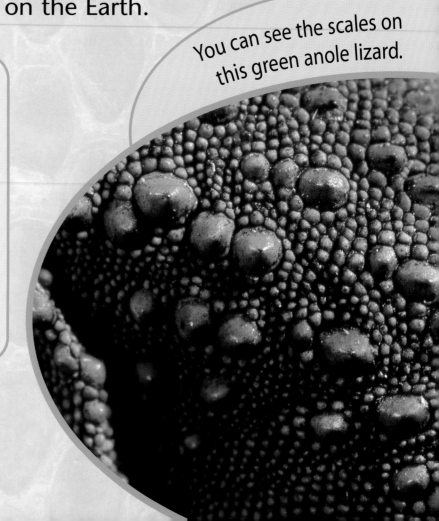

You can see the scales on this green anole lizard.

Difficult pets

There are lots of types of pet lizard. Many lizards that people buy as pets die very quickly. This is because their owners do not realize how difficult lizards are to look after.

You need to think really hard about whether a lizard is the right pet for you. Lizards such as green iguanas need special care. Monitors grow far too big to make a suitable pet. Chameleons are very fragile and can be hurt by handling.

Some lizards grow extremely large and should only be kept in zoos or special reptile homes.

Where Are Lizards From?

Most of the world's lizards are found where there is plenty of sun and heat to keep them warm. Some like **humid** air and others prefer to live where it is dry.

North America is home to lizards such as anoles, geckos, collared lizards, iguanas, and the gila monster. Africa has large monitor lizards and many types of geckos. Australia has geckos, skinks, and many types of monitor lizard, including goannas.

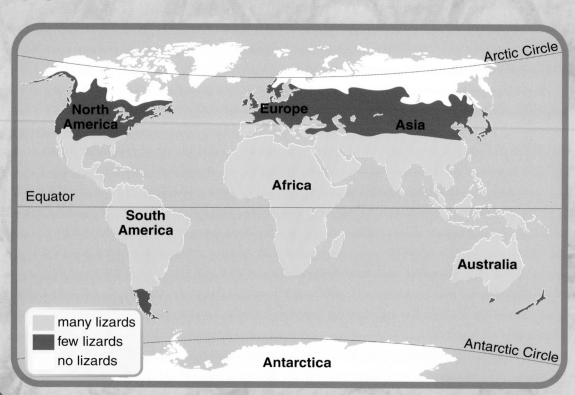

This map shows where lizards live in the world.

Local **reptile** clubs or societies are good places to start looking for a pet lizard. They can give support and advice once you have your pet. You can also ask a veterinarian for advice.

A lizard should be alert and have plenty of energy. It should be clean with clear eyes and nose and healthy looking skin.

Captured in the wild

You should never buy lizards that have been taken from the wild. They may have illnesses or diseases. Many lizards that are caught in the wild do not survive the journey to where they are sold.

Lizard Habitats

In the wild, lizards are found in different kinds of **habitats.** They can live in deserts, in rain forests and jungles, or in rocky places.

Lizards have **adapted** to live in different places. Most lizards need to bask in the sun. The sunlight allows them to absorb **vitamin** D to build healthy skin and bones.

The Nile monitor is a very fast and agile swimmer. It can dive underwater for up to an hour.

Ask an expert what to put in your lizard's vivarium. A desert lizard needs a sand floor, but a rain forest lizard needs leaves and branches.

Lizard homes

Instead of roaming wild, pet lizards usually have to live in a **vivarium.** Vivariums should be made of glass or metal and should not have any sharp edges or wire mesh where lizards might hurt themselves.

Lizards need plenty of fresh air. Stale air can make them ill. Lizards also need heat, but they should always have a place to go to cool down. If your lizard gets too hot, it can die.

Lizard Anatomy

Lizards have small heads, short necks, and long bodies and tails. Most lizards have teeth on both jaws. Some even have teeth on the roof of their mouths!

Color change

Some lizards change color depending on how they are feeling. The green anole is green when warm and relaxed. It turns darker brown when cold or frightened.

Two **species** of lizards are **venomous.** This means that they have a poisonous bite. They are the gila monster from North America, shown here, and the Mexican bearded lizard.

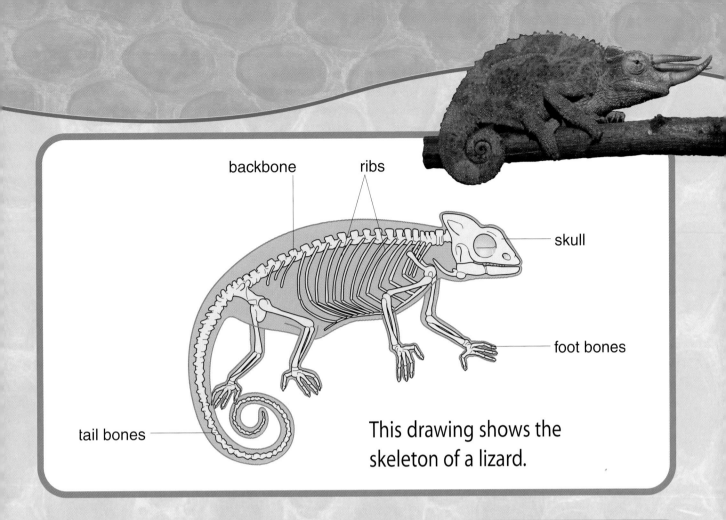

backbone

ribs

skull

foot bones

tail bones

This drawing shows the skeleton of a lizard.

Pet lizards have the same **anatomy,** or body parts, as wild lizards. Your pet lizard has scales, short legs with claws, a tail, and sharp teeth.

Shedding
*Most lizards **shed** their skins. The outer, dead layer falls off leaving a new skin underneath. Most need **humid,** warm air to shed properly.*

Lizards can have patterned scales, like the gila monster. They may be brightly colored like the collared lizard or the sawback agamid. They may have spines like the spiny iguana or the bearded dragon.

13

Senses

A lizard's eyes are usually wide apart and set on either side of its head. It needs all-around vision to watch for dangers. Many lizards, such as chameleons and iguanas, can see in color. In the wild, lizards use skin color to attract a mate or scare away **predators.**

Smelling

A lizard uses its tongue to help it smell things. It flicks its tongue out and **particles** stick to it. Special **cells** on the roof of a lizard's mouth smell the particles. Lizards use their sense of smell to find food and warn of enemies.

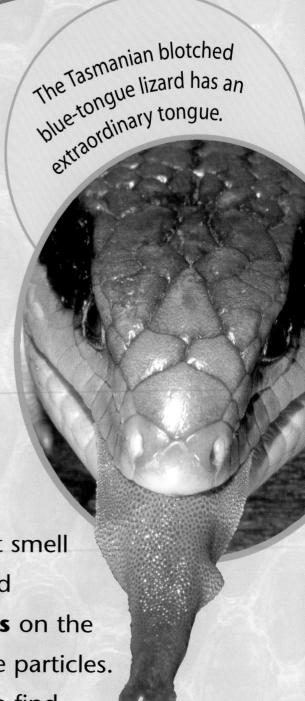

The Tasmanian blotched blue-tongue lizard has an extraordinary tongue.

Your pet lizard may not seem to use its sense of hearing. Lizards have **eardrums** just under the surface of the skin on the sides of their heads. They cannot hear very well.

Special eyes

Some lizards have eyelids and can blink. Others, like geckos, cannot blink. They have clear protective skins over their eyes. They keep their eyes wet by licking them with their tongues.

Some lizards, like chameleons, can use their eyes separately. They can look with one eye in a different direction from the other.

Movement

Some lizards, like chameleons, use their tails to grasp things and to balance.

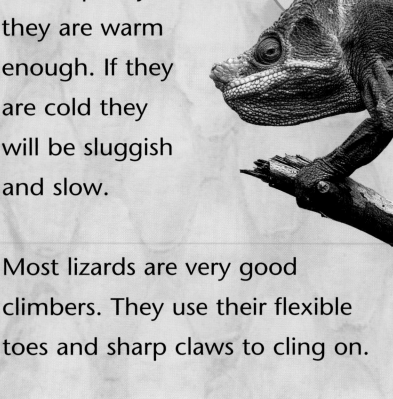

Lizards can only move quickly when they are warm enough. If they are cold they will be sluggish and slow.

Most lizards are very good climbers. They use their flexible toes and sharp claws to cling on.

Some lizards have no legs. They move by using muscles on their bellies. They use their scales to grip the ground.

Flying lizards

The flying dragon lizard lives in South-East Asia and India. It has skin between its legs, which it can spread and use like wings to glide to safety.

Although they cannot run and hunt like wild lizards, pet lizards still need space to move around and exercise in. Lizards need to move to keep their muscles and bones healthy.

Swimming

Some **reptiles,** such as green iguanas, are good swimmers. They need a small pool, like a paddling pool, to swim in. A big, swimming lizard is not the right pet for you if you have not got much space.

Geckos can climb straight up walls and even on the ceiling. They can do this because they have special gripping pads on their toes.

What Do Lizards Eat?

Most wild lizards are **carnivores** or **insectivores**. Some are **omnivores,** which means they eat meat and plants. Others are **herbivores** and eat only plants. Some lizards only need to eat every four to five days.

Monitors and tegus are carnivores. Nile monitors eat fish, crabs, eggs, small animals, and insects.

Green iguanas and chuckwallas are herbivores. Chuckwallas eat mostly leaves and grasses, with some fruit and flowers. Green iguanas eat mainly leaves.

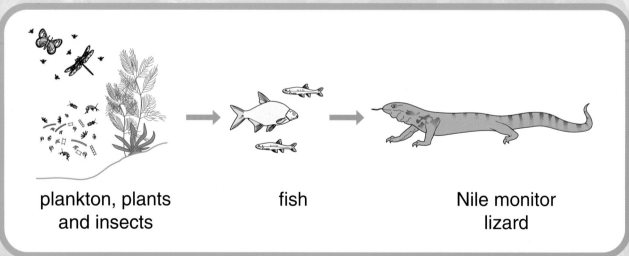

| plankton, plants and insects | fish | Nile monitor lizard |

This is how the Nile monitor fits into a **food chain.**

Lizards may need live food as well as plants and grains.

Carnivorous pet lizards eat dead baby mice, called pinkies, and live insects like crickets and locusts.

Herbivorous pet lizards eat leafy green vegetables like dandelion leaves and flowers. They can also eat grains like wheat, oats, and rice.

Vitamins

*It is difficult to feed pet lizards what they eat in the wild. It is important to help them with extra **vitamins.***

Your lizard should have a clean, full bowl of water at all times. Otherwise it will get ill.

Hunting and Handling

Some lizards hunt food such as small animals and insects. They find their **prey** by lying in wait and watching for movement. Other lizards search out tasty plants to eat. They find their food by smell.

Tongues

Chameleons have amazing tongues. They are sticky and can make a cup shape on the end. A chameleon uses its tongue to catch insects. It shoots its tongue out, swipes the insect, and pulls it into its mouth, all in a split second.

This insect was too slow!

Most lizards do not like being handled.

Most lizards have very strong jaws for hunting. A bite from a big lizard like an iguana can hurt and draw blood. They are not really suitable pets and should only be kept by experts.

Lizards do not enjoy human contact. If you want a pet to cuddle, lizards are not for you.

Watch that tail!

Some lizards, like curly-tails, can "drop" their tails. This is to escape from being caught. They can lose their tails if you grab them suddenly or in the wrong way, so be careful.

Do Lizards Live in Groups?

In the wild, most lizards live alone. Males can fight if they meet.

Body language

Most lizards **communicate** by using body language. Aggressive lizards will open their mouths when they are frightened or angry. Others may puff up or lash their tails.

Many lizards have "beards," or frills around their head and neck area. They can extend these when they want to show-off or threaten another lizard.

The frilled lizard from Australia and New Guinea has a large frill around its neck. It uses this to frighten its enemies.

Dab lizards will usually live happily together.

You can keep some lizards together, even though they would live alone in the wild. Ask an expert before you put lizards together. Males should be separated as soon as they are adults. Otherwise they will fight.

Always check that groups of lizards are not fighting. Bites and scratches can make a lizard very ill.

Unfriendly animals

Lizards are not very friendly animals. They may sometimes come hurrying over to greet you, but only if they think food is coming.

Sleeping

All lizards need sleep. Most lizards are active during the day. This is because their bodies need warmth from the sun to work properly. There are some unusual lizards like geckos, which are active at night.

Green anoles sleep on the tips of leaves. If a **predator** attacks them, the anoles will feel the movement, wake up, and escape.

Lizards usually sleep in gaps in rocks, burrows, or holes in trees and logs.

Hibernation

Most lizards **hibernate** through winter. Hibernation is a very deep sleep. A lizard's body goes into slow-motion and uses very little energy.

In the wild, lizards wake up to hunt and keep warm. Well-kept pet lizards do not need to because they will be fed and kept warm. They rest or sleep most of the time.

Keeping an eye out

Some lizards can sleep with one eye open. Half of their brain is asleep and half of it is working, keeping an eye out for danger. They only do this if they feel scared.

Make sure your lizard has somewhere to hide and sleep. It needs a safe place just as it would in the wild.

Life Cycle of Lizards

Some lizards only live for a short time, while others can live for many years. Bearded dragons live for about 10 years. The Mona ground iguana can live for more than 30 years.

Are lizards good parents?

*Many lizards, like Komodo dragons, lay their eggs and then leave them to hatch on their own. The eggs are buried, but **predators** and even other Komodo dragons often find them and eat them.*

Many lizards lay eggs. Other lizards, like skinks, give birth to live babies.

These are baby collared lizards.

Pet lizards may not live as long as wild lizards. This is because it is very hard to give pet lizards the healthy life they would have in the wild.

Baby lizards

Lizards do not often have babies when kept as pets. But there are some, such as geckos, anoles, and collared lizards that can.

Common Problems

Humans often harm lizards. Wild lizards are caught to sell as pets. Many lizards die before they are sold. Lizard **habitats,** such as rain forests, deserts, and rivers, can be **polluted** or destroyed by industry and farming.

Wild lizards can also suffer from diseases. Most lizards are hunted by **predators** as well. Their predators include other lizards, birds of **prey**, such as eagles, and wild cats.

In danger!
*The following **species** of lizard are **endangered:***
- *Jamaican iguana*
- *Anegada island iguana*
- *Komodo dragon*
- *San Diego coast horned lizard.*

The San Diego coast horned lizard is endangered.

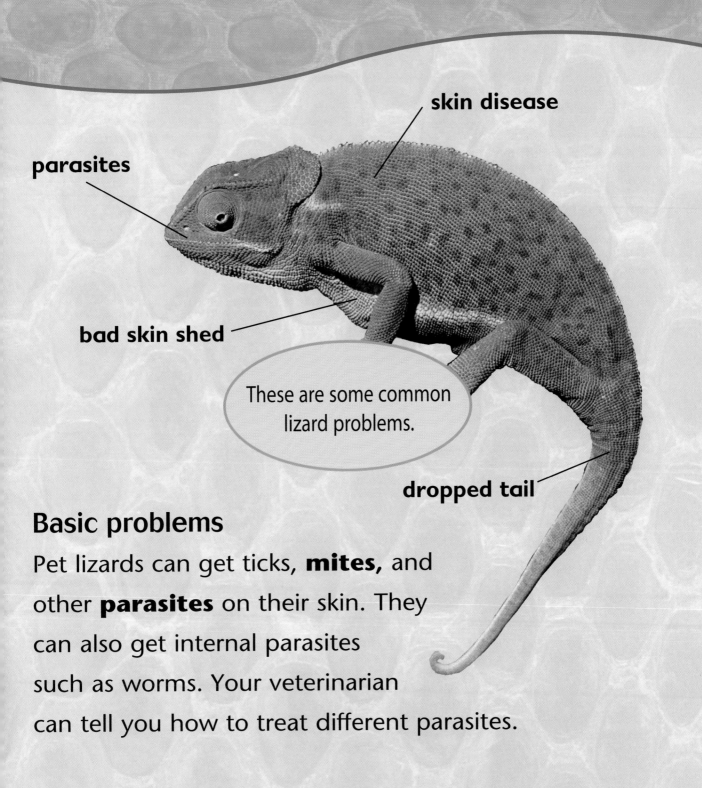

parasites

skin disease

bad skin shed

These are some common lizard problems.

dropped tail

Basic problems

Pet lizards can get ticks, **mites,** and other **parasites** on their skin. They can also get internal parasites such as worms. Your veterinarian can tell you how to treat different parasites.

If your lizard does not get enough sunlight or **ultraviolet** light, it can get very dull and lifeless. It may also get **brittle** bones and eventually die.

Find Out for Yourself

A good owner will always want to learn more about keeping a pet lizard. To find out more information about lizards, you can look in other books and on the Internet.

Books to read

Hernandez-Divers, Sonia. *Geckos.* Chicago: Heinemann Library, 2002.

Manning, David. *Keeping Lizards.* Hauppauge, NY: Barron's Educational Series, 2000.

Using the Internet

Explore the Internet to find out about lizards. Websites can change, so if one of the links below no longer works, do not worry. Use a search engine, such as *www.google.com* or *www.internet4kids.com*. You could try searching using the keywords "lizard," "pet," and "geckos."

Glossary

adapted become used to living in certain conditions

anatomy how the body is made

brittle not strong and can break very easily

carnivore animal that only eats meat

cell smallest part that makes up a living thing

cold-blooded when blood is the same temperature as the air around it

communicate to make yourself understood

eardrum thin layer of skin that allows animals to hear

endangered in danger of dying out or being killed

food chain links between different animals that feed on each other and on plants

habitat where an animal or plant lives

herbivore animal that eats only plants

hibernate go into a deep sleep for winter

humid damp air, containing a lot of water

insectivore animal that only eats insects

mite small parasite that lives on another animal and sucks its blood

omnivore animal that eats meat and plants

parasite tiny animal that lives in or on another animal and feeds off it

particle tiny piece of a substance

pollution making the environment dirty with waste or poisonous chemicals

predator animal that hunts and eats other animals

prey animal that is hunted and eaten by other animals

reptile cold-blooded, scaly animal, like a lizard or snake

shed lose skin or hair

species type of similar animals that can have babies together

ultraviolet type of light

venomous having a poisonous bite

vitamin special chemical that animals need to stay alive

vivarium special tank for keeping lizards in

Index

DATE DUE

NOV 1 3 2007	
JUL 2 9 2008	
JUN 2 3 2009	

BRODART, CO.   Cat. No. 23-221-003